THE ADVENTURES OF LINKA SPOTTER, THE GLOBETROTTER & GEORGE, THE WILD HORSE

From Cuenca to Mongolia

CAROLINA CUBELLS GARCÍA

Cuentacuentos aventurero con kit de ayuda para profes y familias intrépidas.
INGLÉS PRINCIPIANTE

Texto: Carolina Cubells García
Ilustradora: Andrea Rubio García
Prólogo: Miriam Cotillas de la Torre
Revisión texto inglés: Julie-Anne Farman

Edición y maquetación: Cristina Medrano Moreno

Primera edición, 2024
ISBN: 978-84-128302-8-6
Depósito legal: BA-000163-2024
editorialcuatrohojas.com / info@editorialcuatrohojas.com

Dedicado a mis abuelos asturianos,
que me dieron un espacio para ser niña

A través del siguiente código QR podrás acceder a la descarga de actividades complementarias a la lectura.

Prólogo

De Miriam Cotillas de la Torre

¿Qué es aprender? ¡Qué difícil pregunta! Seguramente, diríamos que aprender es adquirir conocimientos. Eso es lo que solemos pensar… aquí. En Occidente, pensamos que las personas nacemos como un recipiente vacío y, conforme nos desarrollamos, de alguna manera, nos vamos llenando de experiencias, conocimientos… y nos vamos construyendo. Eso es lo natural, ¿no? Bueno… En Oriente se piensa lo contrario…, que desarrollarse implica ir perdiendo capas que nos alejan de nuestra verdadera esencia: el miedo a cometer errores, a dar la propia opinión, etcétera, y que cuantas más capas perdemos, más nos acercamos a la verdadera autenticidad, a nuestro verdadero yo. ¡Qué lío! ¿No?

Pues sí, es un lío…, eso está claro. Carolina era una persona más tranquila antes de mezclarse con gente como yo. Yo viajaba bastante, y ella era lo que se decía una persona prudente. En un tiempo récord pasó de pedirme un destino convencional a cabalgar por la estepa mongola en un caballo salvaje, bucear en el Índico, vivir unas elecciones incendiarias en África, quedarnos en un glaciar con las llaves dentro del coche sin poder salir y mil aventuras y desventuras que no caben aquí. Y, claro…, todo eso… le ha pasado factura.

Eso le pasa a mi amiga: que desde que viaja tanto por países tan dispares y trabaja en escuelas rurales con alumnado de todas las edades, procedencias y características en la misma clase, tiene la cabeza hecha un galimatías. Sus intentos de acercar la inmensa diversidad del mundo a la tremenda diversidad infantil a través de la vasta diversidad lingüística se parecen a algo así como intentar la cuadratura del círculo.

Aún recuerdo las conversaciones en las que trataba de convencerme, entusiasmada, de que sería un negocio genial fletar una furgoneta interactiva donde montar una academia de inglés itinerante en la cual hacer actividades inmersivas en inglés para acercar el idioma y las experiencias internacionales a los pueblos remotos de quince habitantes de la Serranía y la Alcarria de Cuenca, en los cuales, con un poco de suerte, había un/a niño/a o un par…, mientras yo observaba con los ojos como platos pensando en la cantidad de gastos que tendría una empresa así, sin saber cómo expresarle las cuentas para no apagar la luz de sus ojos mientras enumeraba la cantidad de actividades que se podrían llevar a cabo… Carolina es una mujer de utopías, pero como bien decía Eduardo Galeano: «La utopía está en el horizonte. Camino dos pasos, ella se aleja dos pasos y el horizonte se corre diez pasos más allá. Entonces, ¿para qué sirve la utopía? Para eso, sirve para caminar».

Pues eso es lo que consigue ella, caminar. Al final, de un modo u otro consigue acercar el planeta en inglés a más personas cada vez, mientras intenta llegar a la utopía de que sea a todo el mundo… Y de ahí surgen resultados… maravillosos, la verdad…, como este recurso.

¿Y de qué va todo esto? Pues, básicamente, este libro reúne un poco todo esto que la cabezota de mi amiga ha estado intentando: es una herramienta basada en un cuentacuentos en el que podremos cabalgar junto a Linka Spotter y su caballo salvaje (mongol, cómo no), George. Ambos nos llevan por la magia de los paraísos naturales del mundo mientras descubrimos y practicamos la lengua inglesa. Se trata de que podamos lanzarnos a imaginar y soñar, pero, sobre todo, de que estemos tan pendientes de la historia que no nos preocupemos de la posibilidad de cometer errores, de que perdamos el miedo y, simplemente, como si estuviéramos en Mongolia con caballos que no entienden de doma, galopáramos siendo quienes somos y disfrutáramos sin más, sin preocuparnos de normas. Lo que más me ha gustado es que, de alguna forma, la actividad se enfoca en la comprensión, en motivar el avance, y evita frustraciones gratuitas que bloqueen las ganas de aprender. Yo, que no sé montar a caballo, que no conozco las instrucciones que hay que darles, me sentí libre en Mongolia, porque allí se podía de alguna forma cabalgar con la intuición. Era cuestión de comunicación. Quizá haya sentido algo parecido con esta actividad poniéndome en la piel de alguien que no sepa inglés. Siento que lo que pretende es focalizarse en descubrir el mundo desde la curiosa y astuta mirada infantil, haciendo que la lengua parezca algo circunstancial. Es un poco… como llevar Mongolia a Estados Unidos, pasando por Cuenca. Como hacer una paella al estilo africano…, algo muy… Carolina. Pues eso. Hay que conocerla para entender la descripción. Simplemente me encanta.

Tengo que reconocer que, aun siendo una persona adulta con un alto nivel de inglés, he disfrutado mucho del cuento (sí, también tenemos ganas de soñar y capas que quitarnos), pero realmente habría sido maravilloso poder disponer de un recurso así en el colegio o haberlo podido usar en familia cuando era niña. Ahora ya existe, así que ¡vamos a disfrutarlo!

Objetivos

The Adventures of Linka Spotter, the Globetrotter & George, the Wild Horse es una herramienta didáctica basada en un cuentacuentos, que utiliza la lengua inglesa para describir las aventuras de una niña y un caballo a través de distintos parques naturales del planeta, e incluye actividades en las que se usan las destrezas básicas relacionadas con el aprendizaje lingüístico. Este recurso es muy versátil y se puede aplicar tanto en clase por docentes como en casa por familias implicadas en el proceso de aprendizaje, aprovechando la curiosidad por el inglés.

El propósito principal de esta actividad es aprender mediante la diversión, despertar la curiosidad y dejar volar la imaginación de la mente infantil, ávida de historias y aventuras. Aprovechando ese deseo de soñar, surge el segundo propósito: crear algo integrador, novedoso, con vocación de herramienta unificada, un recurso pensado para servir de ayuda en aulas unitarias o multinivel a la hora de implementar el plan de lectura, pero tan versátil que puede adaptarse no solo a este fin, sino a cualquier entorno escolar o incluso a una agradable actividad en familia. Debido a la existencia de aquellos Centros Rurales Agrupados (CRA) en los que se imparten distintos niveles educativos de manera simultánea en una misma aula por el escaso alumnado, nace la necesidad de contar con materiales que puedan tener un uso común. Este recurso puede facilitar tanto la labor docente como la interacción y convivencia entre el alumnado de los distintos niveles. Así mismo, dicha realidad multinivel se puede ver reflejada en cualquier aula ordinaria, compuesta por una diversidad creciente de estudiantes cuyas diferencias individuales deben ser atendidas y en las que todo el alumnado debe encontrar respuesta educativa, motivación y un ambiente propicio para el desarrollo de sus capacidades.

De igual manera, y como tercer propósito, este recurso pretende maximizar la adquisición de conocimientos a través de la metodología AICLE (Aprendizaje Integrado de Contenidos y Lenguas Extranjeras o conocido como CLIL en inglés *(Content Language Integrated Learning)*, de manera que el alumnado adquiera otras destrezas relacionadas con conocimiento del medio, valores, etcétera, a través del área de inglés como lengua extranjera, desarrollando en todo momento y mediante el juego las habilidades comunicativas de la lengua inglesa.

Además de lo ya mencionado, este pequeño cuentacuentos contribuye a la consecución de toda una serie de retos educativos:

- Incluir la gamificación en el proceso de enseñanza-aprendizaje, generando una experiencia más motivadora.
- Servir de herramienta para establecer un sistema de normas.
- Establecer una rutina de lectura que fomente los hábitos, la comunicación y el plurilingüismo.
- Fomentar el refuerzo positivo ante el buen comportamiento.
- Incentivar la recompensa del esfuerzo.
- Fomentar el respeto por las diferentes culturas (interculturalidad).
- Inculcar responsabilidad en el uso del material.

- Involucrar a las familias en el proceso de enseñanza-aprendizaje.
- Transmitir la motivación por el aprendizaje del inglés como lengua extranjera.
- Poner en práctica una serie de competencias tales como la digital (al llevar a cabo una investigación online para averiguar respuestas a los distintos sets de preguntas) o, de manera paralela, cualquiera de las otras (plurilingüe, personal, aprender a aprender, ciudadana, etcétera), todas ellas igualmente importantes a la hora de contribuir al desarrollo del individuo en su totalidad.

Este recurso está orientado a una edad que puede oscilar entre los seis y los nueve años, pudiéndose llevar a cabo las adaptaciones necesarias en los sets de preguntas o las actividades relacionas con la lectura a las que se puede acceder mediante el código QR, según las necesidades del alumnado en cada momento.

ESTRUCTURA Y CONTENIDO DE The Adventures of Linka Spotter, the Globetrotter & George, the Wild Horse

The Adventures of Linka Spotter, the Globetrotter & George, the Wild Horse es un pequeño cuento interactivo donde la rima y las estructuras repetitivas nos acompañan en la lectura para favorecer la producción de lenguaje por parte del alumnado y conseguir que este pueda hacer predicciones sobre lo que vendrá a continuación, así como facilitar la interiorización de estructuras gramaticales de manera inconsciente. Esto pretende crear un ambiente de aprendizaje en el que el alumnado se sienta seguro y capaz de hacer contribuciones orales, minimizando la atención al error. Al fin y al cabo, perder el miedo a cometer errores es clave para atreverse a avanzar en el aprendizaje de una lengua extranjera.

Se trata de una curiosa y aventurera niña de ocho años afincada en Cuenca que, junto con su inseparable compañero, un caballo salvaje de Mongolia, nos acompañarán a través de una serie de fascinantes parques nacionales del mundo. Comenzarán en el parque natural de la Serranía de Cuenca, debiendo contestar para avanzar un set de preguntas que considere oportuno el/la docente o la persona responsable de dirigir la actividad. Tanto los personajes como los parajes cumplen el propósito de subrayar valores esenciales en nuestra sociedad, ya sea la colaboración, la inclusión, la conciencia cultural, así como el respeto por el medioambiente, entre otros.

Las preguntas sugeridas al final del cuento contienen una revisión, tanto de estructuras gramaticales como de un banco de vocabulario de alta frecuencia. La dinámica se puede realizar consultando la pregunta correspondiente al final del cuento o imprimiendo las tarjetas a través del código QR. A través de este, se pueden descargar de manera gratuita una serie de materiales complementarios para trabajar con la lectura. En cuanto al resto, se deja a la imaginación de cada cual, de manera que las ideas personales generan una batería casi infinita de combinaciones.

El aprendizaje no entiende de género, edad ni clase social. Tampoco tiene fin, salvo el que quiera cada cual.

¡A disfrutar!

Hello!

My name is Linka Spotter, the Globetrotter. I am an 8-year-old girl who attends 3rd level of Primary Education in a super school next to **Serranía de Cuenca Natural Park**. I love horses, sports and travelling around the world. What about you?

Do you want to know about my adventures? If so, continue reading and use your imagination to join my story!

* * *

It is 10 o'clock in the morning on a sunny Sunday. I am walking next to the river while I listen to the birds ("tweet tweet"). Suddenly, I see a horse drinking water from the river.

"Wow! It is so beautiful!"

I call it (TEACHER MAKES NOISE), but the horse gets scared. Then, I sit down and wait on a rock. After 5 minutes, it stands next to me and to my surprise, it starts talking to me!!

"Hello! Where am I?" says the horse looking confused.

"We are at Serranía de Cuenca Natural Park. Why? Didn't you know?"

"Oh…Let me tell you…. My name is George, the wild horse. Last Monday I got angry with my family and I ran away. Now, I want to find my family but I don't know where they are" says the horse looking sad.

"Where is your house, George? Where are you from?" asks Linka.

"I live in a National Park like this one where there are beautiful mountains, eagles and lots of wild horses that run free like me".

"I want to help you! Let's meet here on Monday at 6 p.m. I'll find a solution!"

"Ok! Thank you, Linka!"

"You're welcome!"

* * *

On Monday morning, I ask my super teacher for help.

"Teacher, can I ask you a question?"

"Sure Linka! Go ahead, please!"

"Teacher…where can I find a National Park where there are beautiful mountains, eagles and wild horses that run free?"

"That's a good question Linka! Remember what I always say: When we don't know something, we look…"

"In a book!" says Linka.

"Exactly! Here is a travel book that will help you."

"Thank you, teacher!"

"You're welcome!"

Then, I have a look at my teacher's travel book.

"Oh, no! There are many National Parks with beautiful mountains, eagles and wild horses that run free! But…where does George live? We need help!"

It is Monday at 6 p.m. next to the river at Serranía de Cuenca Natural Park.

"Hey George! Good news! I have a National Parks book to find your family!"

"Wow, Linka, that's a great idea!"

"It is! Now, let's open the book and press the magic button!"

Suddenly, a happy Nightingale comes out from the book and says:

"Hi! Can I help you?"

"Yes, please! We are looking for my friend's family; they live in a National Park where there are beautiful mountains, eagles and wild horses that run free, just like George, the wild horse."

"Ok! Then, go to Connemara National Park" says the nightingale.

"Oh! But, where is it?"

"It's in Ireland…Don't worry! I'll take you there! But first, you have to answer a question…"

"Super!"

QUESTION 1 (see annex I)

"Brilliant!"

"Thank you, Nightingale!"

"You're welcome! Off we go!"

Then, we arrive at **Connemara National Park**, in Ireland. We open the book and press the magic button. Suddenly, a sleepy Mouse comes out from the book and says:

"Welcome to Connemara National Park! Can I help you?"

"Yes, please! We are looking for my friend's family; they live in a National Park where there are beautiful mountains, eagles and wild horses that run free, just like George, the wild horse. Are we in the right place?" says Linka.

"Well, here there are beautiful mountains, eagles and wild horses that run free, but they are not like George. Go to Vatnajökull National Park!"

"Oh! But, where is it?"

"It's in Iceland…Don't worry! I'll take you there! But first, you have to answer a question…"

"Super!"

QUESTION 2 (see annex I)

"Awesome!"

"Thank you, Mouse!"

"You're welcome! Off we go!"

Then, we arrive at **Vatnajökull National Park**, in Iceland. We open the book and press the magic button. Suddenly a proud Goat comes out from the book and says:

"Welcome to Vatnajökull National Park! Can I help you?"

"Yes, please! We are looking for my friend's family; they live in a National Park where there are beautiful mountains, eagles and wild horses that run free, just like George, the wild horse. Are we in the right place?" says Linka.

"Well, here there are beautiful mountains, eagles and wild horses that run free, but they are not like George. Go to Jostedalsbreen National Park!"

"Oh! But, where is it?"

"It's in Norway…Don't worry! I'll take you there! But first, you have to answer a question…"

"Super!"

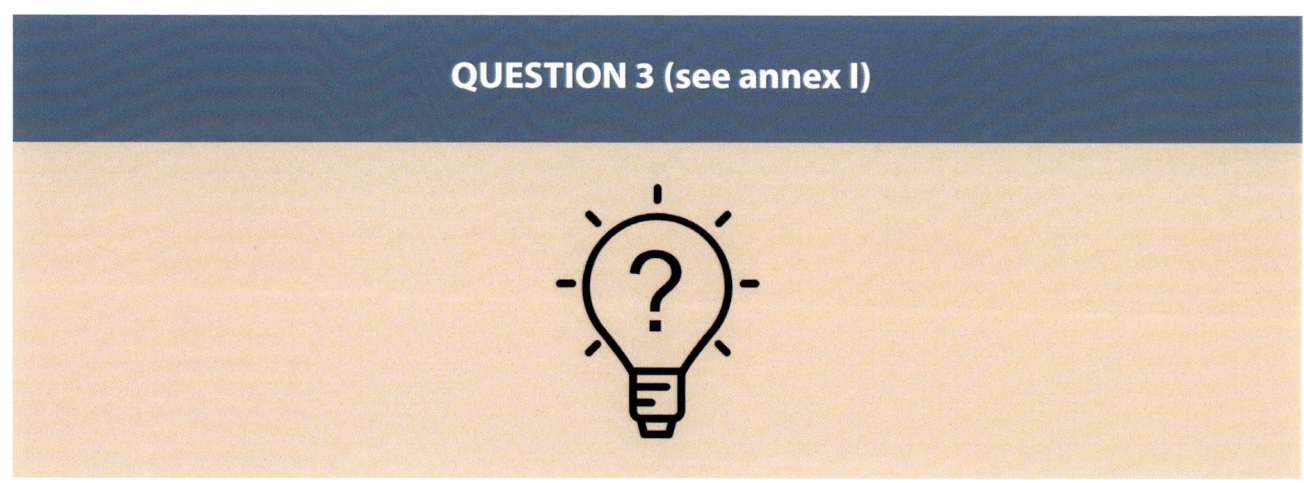

QUESTION 3 (see annex I)

"Fantastic!"

"Thank you, Goat!"

"You're welcome! Off we go!"

Then, we arrive at **Jostedalsbreen National Park**, in Norway. We open the book and press the magic button. Suddenly, a shy **Lynx** comes out from the book and says:

"Welcome to Jostedalsbreen National Park! Can I help you?"

"Yes, please! We are looking for my friend's family; they live in a National Park where there are beautiful mountains, eagles and wild horses that run free, just like George, the wild horse. Are we in the right place?" says Linka.

"Well, here there are beautiful mountains, eagles and wild horses that run free, but they are not like George. Go to Yosemite National Park!"

"Oh! But, where is it?"

"It's in the USA…Don't worry! I'll take you there! But first, you have to answer a question…"

"Super!"

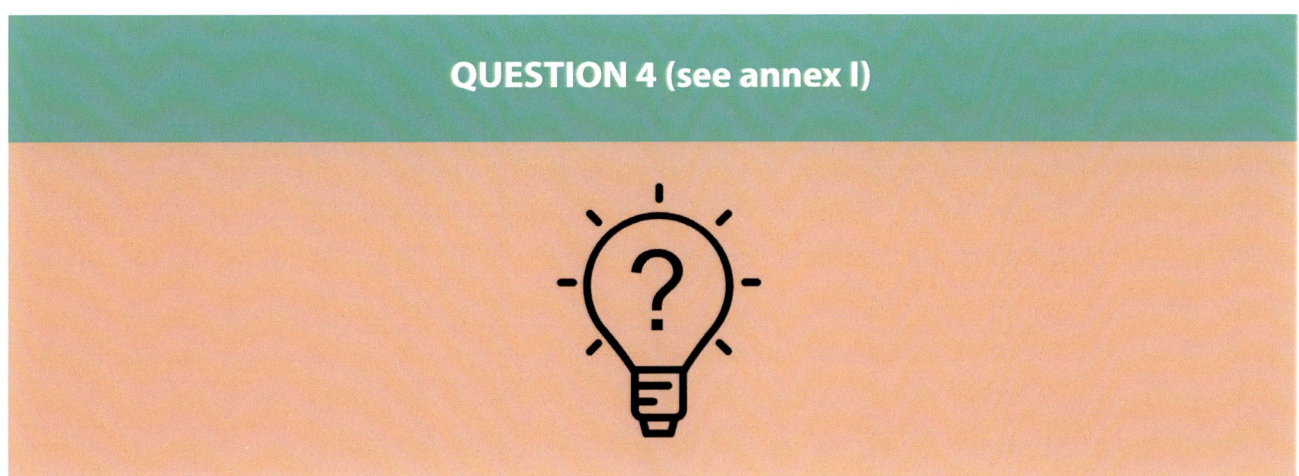

QUESTION 4 (see annex I)

"Wonderful!"

"Thank you, Lynx!"

"You're welcome! Off we go!"

Then, we arrive at **Yosemite National Park**, in the USA. We open the book and press the magic button. Suddenly, a mad **Bear** comes out from the book and says:

"Welcome to Yosemite National Park! Can I help you?

"Yes, please! We are looking for my friend's family; they live in a National Park where there are beautiful mountains, eagles and wild horses that run free, just like George, the wild horse. Are we in the right place?" says Linka.

"Well, as you can see, here there are beautiful mountains, eagles and wild horses that run free, but they are not like George. Go to Yellowstone National Park!"

"Oh! But, where is it?"

"It's here! In the USA…Don't worry! I'll take you there! But first, you have to answer a question…"

"Super!"

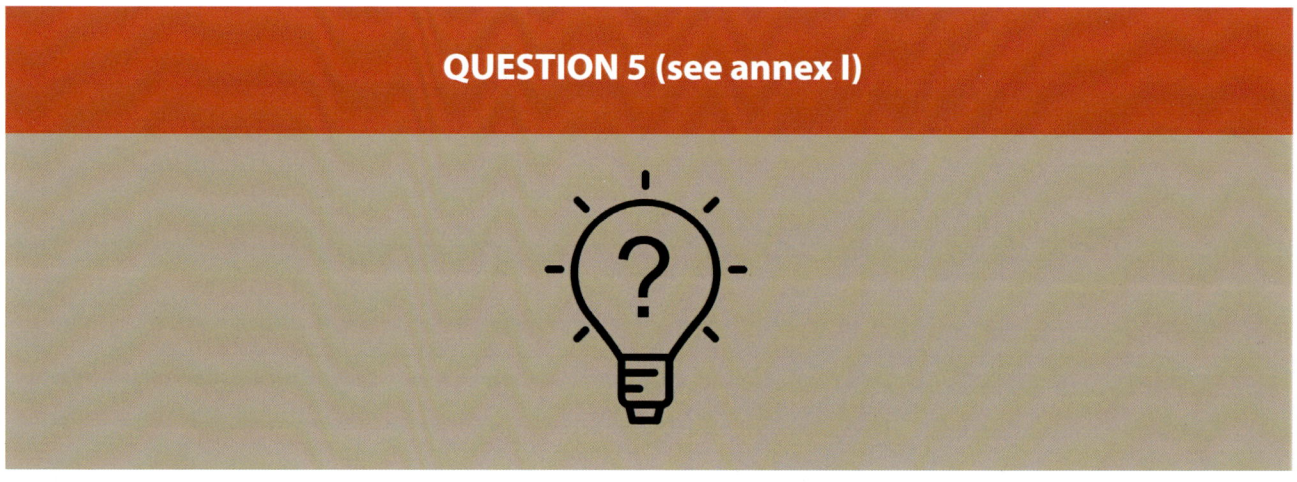

QUESTION 5 (see annex I)

"Good job!"

"Thank you, Bear!"

"You're welcome! Off we go!"

Then, we arrive at **Yellowstone National Park**, in the USA. We open the book and press the magic button. Suddenly, a surprised Coyote comes out from the book and says:

"Welcome to Yellowstone National Park! Can I help you?"

"Yes, please! We are looking for my friend's family; they live in a National Park where there are beautiful mountains, eagles and wild horses that run free, just like George, the wild horse. Are we in the right place?" says Linka.

"Well, here there are beautiful mountains, eagles and wild horses that run free, but they are not like George. Go to Banff National Park!"

"Oh! But, where is it?"

"It's in Canada…Don't worry! I'll take you there! But first, you have to answer a question…"

"Super!"

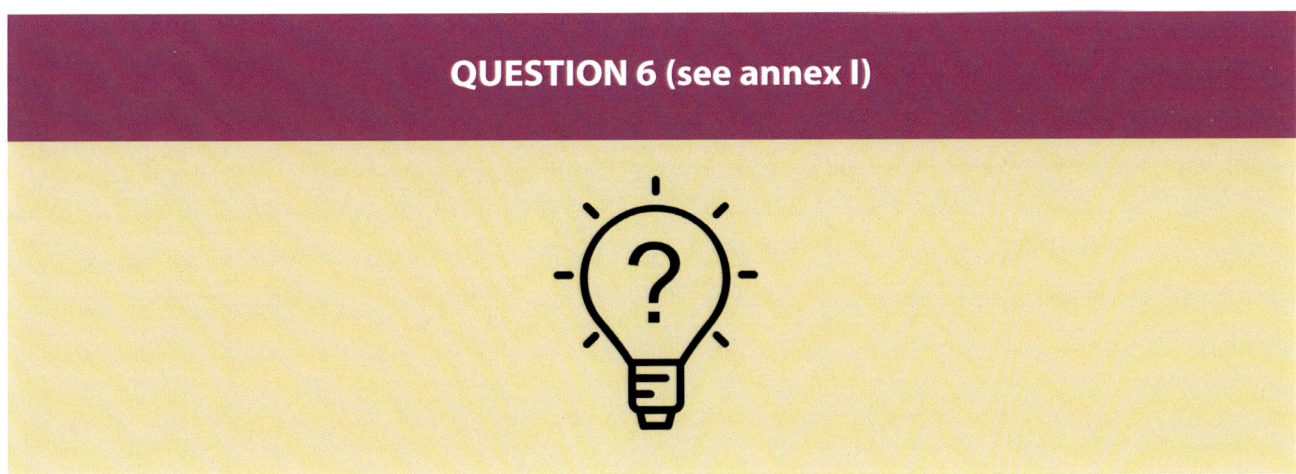

QUESTION 6 (see annex I)

"Spectacular!"

"Thank you, Coyote!"

"You're welcome! Off we go!"

Then, we arrive at **Banff National Park**, in Canada. We open the book and press the magic button. Suddenly, a calm **Deer** comes out from the book and says:

"Welcome to Banff National Park! Can I help you?"

"Yes, please! We are looking for my friend's family; they live in a National Park where there are beautiful mountains, eagles and wild horses that run free, just like George, the wild horse. Are we in the right place?" says Linka.

"Well, here there are beautiful mountains, eagles and wild horses that run free, but they are not like George. Go to Torres del Paine National Park!"

"Oh! But, where is it?"

"It's in Chile… Don't worry! I'll take you there! But first, you have to answer a question…"

"Super!"

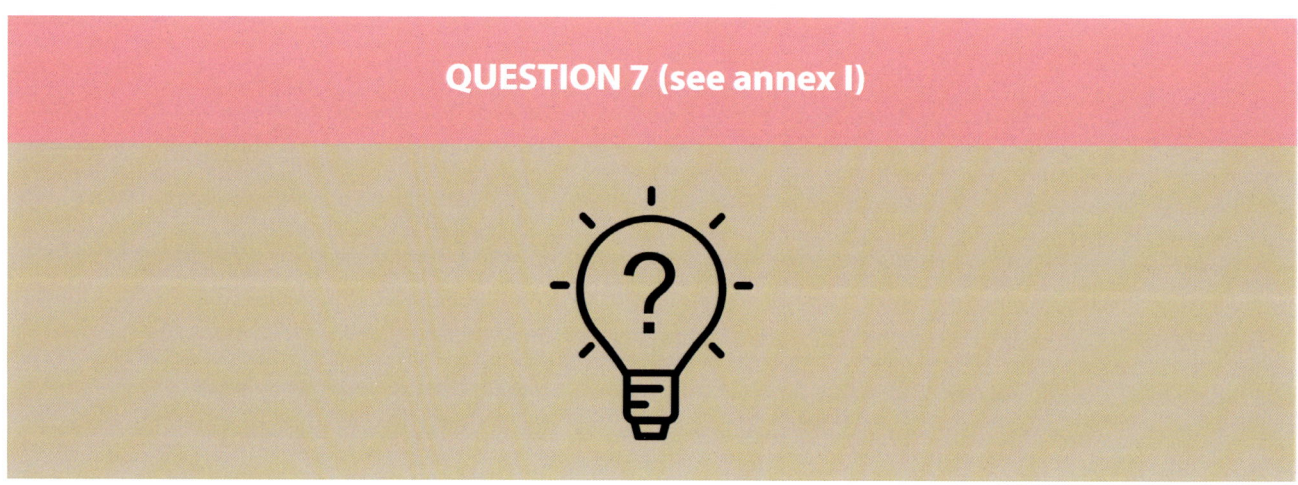

QUESTION 7 (see annex I)

"Magnificent!"

"Thank you, Deer!"

"You're welcome! Off we go!"

Then, we arrive at **Torres del Paine National Park**, in Chile. We open the book and press the magic button. Suddenly, a nervous Ant comes out from the book and says:

"Welcome to Torres del Paine National Park! Can I help you?"

"Yes, please! We are looking for my friend's family; they live in a National Park where there are beautiful mountains, eagles and wild horses that run free, just like George, the wild horse. Are we in the right place?" says Linka.

"Well, here there are beautiful mountains, eagles and wild horses that run free, but they are not like George. Go to Uluru National Park!"

"Oh! But, where is it?"

"It's in Australia…Don't worry! I'll take you there! But first, you have to answer a question…"

"Super!"

QUESTION 8 (see annex I)

"Very well done!"

"Thank you, Ant!"

"You're welcome! Off we go!"

Then, we arrive at **Uluru National Park**, in Australia. We open the book and press the magic button. Suddenly, a scared **Jackal** comes out from the book and says:

"Welcome to Uluru National Park! Can I help you?"

"Yes, please! We are looking for my friend's family; they live in a National Park where there are beautiful mountains, eagles and wild horses that run free, just like George, the wild horse. Are we in the right place?" says Linka.

"Well, here there are beautiful mountains, eagles and wild horses that run free, but they are not like George. Go to Fiordland National Park!"

"Oh! But, where is it?"

"It's in New Zealand…Don't worry! I'll take you there! But first, you have to answer a question…"

"Super!"

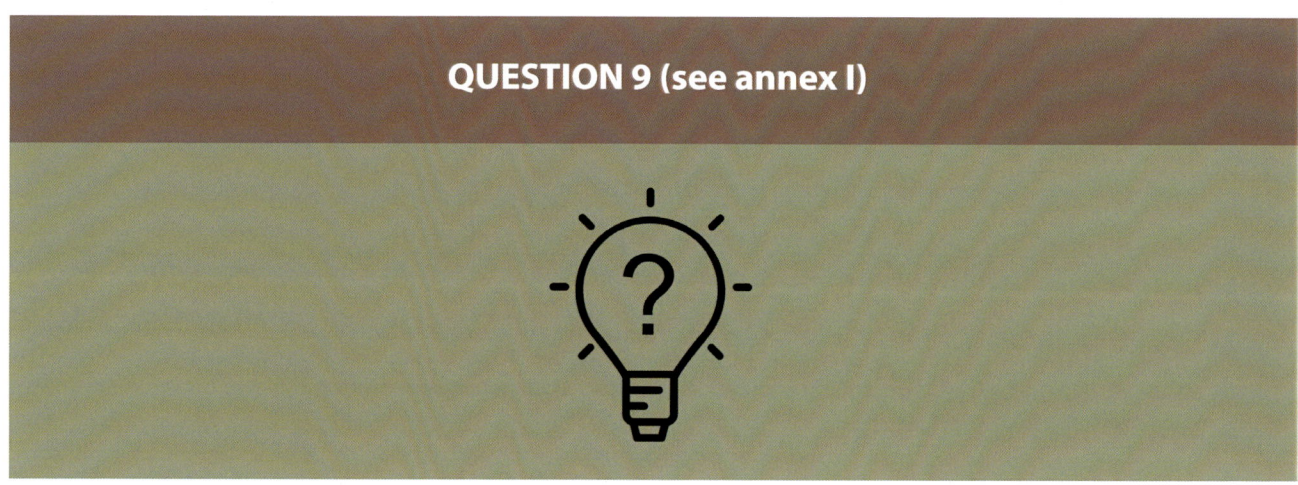

QUESTION 9 (see annex I)

"Outstanding!"

"Thank you, Jackal!"

"You're welcome! Off we go!"

Then, we arrive at Fiordland National Park, in New Zealand. We open the book and press the magic button. Suddenly, a joyful Kangaroo comes out from the book and says:

"Welcome to Fiordland National Park! Can I help you?"

"Yes, please! We are looking for my friend's family; they live in a National Park where there are beautiful mountains, eagles and wild horses that run free, just like George, the wild horse. Are we in the right place?" says Linka.

"Well, here there are beautiful mountains, eagles and wild horses that run free, but they are not like George. Go to Masai Mara National Park!"

"Oh! But, where is it?"

"It's in Kenya…Don't worry! I'll take you there! But first, you have to answer a question…"

"Super!"

QUESTION 10 (see annex I)

"Impressive!"

"Thank you, Kangaroo!"

"You're welcome! Off we go!"

Then, we arrive at **Masai Mara National Park**, in Kenya. We open the book and press the magic button. Suddenly, a playful **Impala** comes out from the book and says:

"Welcome to Masai Mara National Park! Can I help you?"

"Yes, please! We are looking for my friend's family; they live in a National Park where there are beautiful mountains, eagles and wild horses that run free, just like George, the wild horse. Are we in the right place?" says Linka.

"Well, here there are beautiful mountains, eagles and wild horses that run free, but they are not like George. Go to Hustai National Park!"

"Oh! But, where is it?"

"It's in Mongolia…Don't worry! I'll take you there! But first, you have to answer a question…"

"Super!"

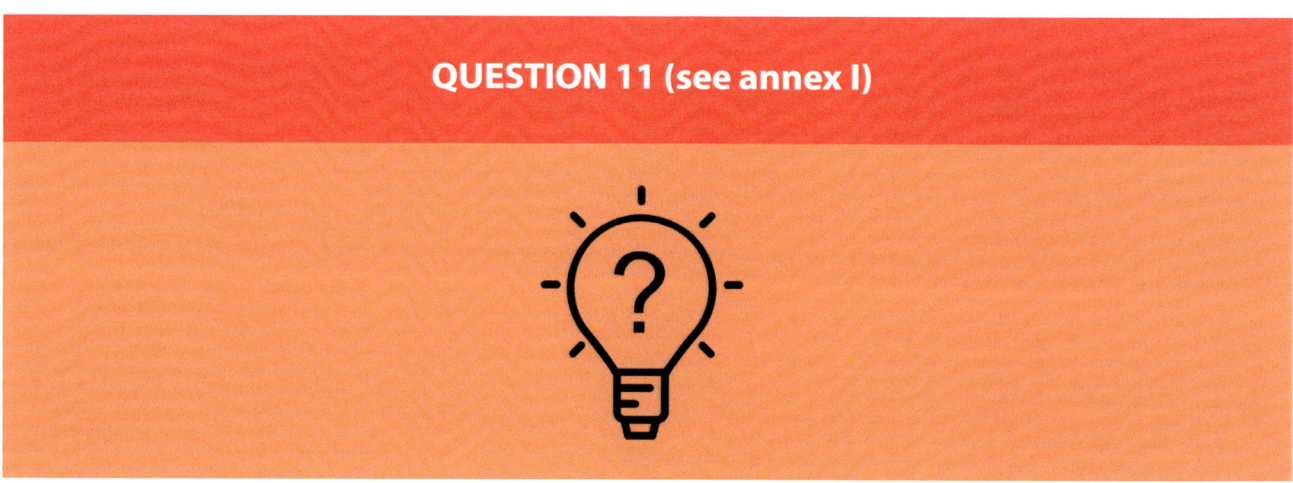

QUESTION 11 (see annex I)

"Stunning!"

"Thank you, Impala!"

"You're welcome! Off we go!"

Then, we arrive at **Hustai National Park**, in Mongolia. We open the book and press the magic button. Suddenly, a brave **Eagle** comes out from the book and says:

"Welcome to Hustai National Park! Can I help you?"

"Yes, please! We are looking for my friend's family; they live in a National Park where there are beautiful mountains, eagles and wild horses that run free, just like George, the wild horse. Are we in the right place?" says Linka.

"Well, here there are beautiful mountains, eagles and wild horses that run free, exactly like George!

"George! We are finally at home!" says Linka.

"Neigh, neigh, I am so happy now! Look! That's my family!" says George.

Then, George gets together with his family and says sorry for disappearing.

"I promise not to run away anymore! Now, let me tell you about my adventures around the world, but first I'll say goodbye to Linka" says George.

"Sure, George!" says George's mom.

"Thank you for your help, Linka! Have fun on your way back home!"

"Sure, George! I am so happy that you are with your family! And now I know so many National Parks! Remember…nature and animals helped us! Now it's our turn to treat nature as a friend!

"Absolutely! And I will also treat children as friends!" says George.

"Thank you, mother nature!" both said.

"Bye bye, George!"

"Bye bye, Linka!"

Home, sweet home.

Then, I press the magic button to go back home with the Eagle's help…

ANNEX 1 – SAMPLE QUESTIONS & ANSWERS

SET OF QUESTIONS 1

FEELINGS, MONTHS, NUMBERS, TIME (o'clock) & TO BE (affirmative):

1. What is the opposite of sad? HAPPY
2. Are your classmates friendly? YES, THEY ARE.
3. This is how I feel before my birthday: EXCITED
4. This is how I feel after doing exercise: TIRED
5. How many months are there in a year? TWELVE / 12
6. What months are there in spring? MARCH, APRIL, MAY AND JUNE
7. What months are there in summer? JUNE, JULY, AUGUST AND SEPTEMBER
8. What months are there in autumn? SEPTEMBER, OCTOBER, NOVEMBER AND DECEMBER
9. What months are there in winter? DECEMBER, JANUARY, FEBRUARY AND MARCH
10. When is your birthday? STUDENTS' OWN ANSWERS
11. What time is it? A) I AM HAPPY; B) IT IS 2 O'CLOCK; C) SHE IS SAD

SET OF QUESTIONS 2

ALPHABET, HOUSEHOLD ITEMS, PREPOSITIONS OF PLACE & TO BE (negative):

1. Can you spell your name? _ _ _ _ _
2. Where can you find a coffee table? A) IN THE LIVING ROOM; B) ON THE LIVING ROOM; C) NEXT TO THE TOILET
3. Is a table made of cardboard? NO, IT'S NOT! It is made of metal and plastic!
4. What do you use for sitting down next to your family in the living room? A SOFA
5. Is a coffee table made of paper? NO, IT'S NOT! It is made of wood!
6. What is the opposite of on? UNDER
7. Is a fridge made of wood? NO, IT'S NOT! It is made of metal!
8. What is the opposite of in front of? BEHIND
9. Where do you place the books in a library? IN THE BOOKCASE
10. Where can you keep your clothes? IN A WARDROBE
11. What word can you make using the first letter of each of the following words? Cat, Under, Red, Ten, Are, In, Next, Shower

SET OF QUESTIONS 3

DESCRIBING PEOPLE, TO HAVE (affirmative) & TO BE (interrogative):

1. What is the opposite of tall? **SHORT**
2. Say a synonym of intelligent: **SMART/CLEVER**
3. What have you got in your pencil case? **I'VE GOT A PENCIL, A SHARPENER, A RULER...**
4. Ask me if I am shy: **ARE YOU SHY?**
5. Can you spell confident? **C-O-N-F-I-D-E-N-T**
6. People who help others are…**KIND**
7. Complete the sentence: MY SISTER _ _ _/_ _ _ FRECKLES. **HAS GOT**
8. When you treat everyone like a friend, you are…**FRIENDLY**
9. Complete the sentence: Where are my _ _ _ _ _ _ _? I can't see anything! **GLASSES**
10. Unscramble the letters to make a new word out of them: N N U F Y. **FUNNY**
11. Can you describe Linka Spotter? **STUDENTS' OWN ANSWERS**

SET OF QUESTIONS 4

POSSESSIONS, NUMBERS (13-30), TO HAVE GOT (interrogative) & POSSESSIVE (saxon genitive):

1. Whose book is this? **IT'S THE TEACHER'S BOOK / IT'S YOUR BOOK**
2. Ask me if I have any brothers or sisters: **HAVE YOU GOT ANY BROTHERS OR SISTERS?**
3. Can you count from 30 to 13 backwards? **30, 29, 28…**
4. What do I need to cut a piece of paper? **SCISSORS**
5. Complete the sentence: IT IS NOT MY RUBBER; IT BELONGS TO MY SISTER: IT IS MY _ _ _ _ _ _ _ _/_ _ _ _ _ _. **SISTER'S RUBBER**
6. What do I need to colour a picture? **COLOUR PENCILS**
7. Finish the sentence: WHEN WE DON'T KNOW SOMETHING WE LOOK IN A _ _ _ _. **BOOK**
8. Where do you keep your pencil case? **A) IN MY SCHOOL BAG**; B) ON THE TEACHER'S DESK; C) UNDER MY FRIEND'S CHAIR
9. Can you spell 'ruler'? **R-U-L-E-R**
10. What do I need to stick a piece of paper? **GLUE**
11. If I want to erase what I write, what should I write with? A) A PEN; B) A PAIR OF GLASSES; **C) A PENCIL**

SET OF QUESTIONS 5

PETS/TO HAVE GOT (negative) & VERB TO BE (short answers):

1. What kind of animal is George? **(A) HORSE**. Can you spell it? _ _ _ _ _ _
2. What does George move to get rid of flies? **TAIL**
3. Have turtles got whiskers? **NO, THEY HAVEN'T! THEY HAVE SHELLS**
4. What word can you make using the first letter of each of the following words? **B**rown, **E**ar, **A**nimal, **K**iwi **BEAK**
5. What animals have got a beak? **BIRDS**
6. Are parrots scary? A) YES, THEY ARE; **B) NO, THEY AREN'T**
7. Have you got any pets? **YES, I HAVE/NO, I HAVEN'T**
8. Has a cat got a beak? **NO, IT HASN'T. IT'S GOT WHISKERS**
9. What animals have got scales? **FISH**
10. Name 3 animals with fur: **SAMPLE ANSWER: DOGS, CATS AND FOXES**
11. Are butterflies colourful? **A) YES, THEY ARE**; B) NO, THEY AREN'T

SET OF QUESTIONS 6

DAILY ROUTINES, TIME (half past) & SEQUENCING (first, then, & finally):

1. What do you usually do around 11 o'clock p.m.? **SAMPLE ANSWER: I USUALLY GO TO BED**
2. What do you do first? A) FIRST, I HAVE LUNCH; **B) FIRST, I HAVE BREAKFAST;** C) FIRST, I HAVE DINNER
3. Complete the sentence: I usually study at _ _ _ _ past five. **HALF**
4. What time do you do your homework? **AT (STUDENTS' OWN ANSWERS)**
5. What is the first thing you do in the morning? **SAMPLE ANSWER: I WAKE UP**
6. Complete the sentence: I _ _ _ _ _ MY TEETH 3 TIMES A DAY. **BRUSH**
7. Choose the most appropriate answer for the following question: What time do you go to school? **A) AT HALF PAST EIGHT**; B) AT HALF PAST NINE; C) AT HALF PAST TEN
8. Unscramble the underlined letters to make a new word out of them: I DO OPSRST EVERYDAY **SPORTS**
9. Complete the sentence: THERE IS A '_ _ O_ _ _' IN THE BATHROOM **SHOWER**
10. Choose the correct order of these actions by using FIRST, THEN and FINALLY: MEET FRIENDS/GO TO SCHOOL/DO HOMEWORK. **STUDENTS' OWN ANSWERS**
11. Complete the sentence: I usually have milk with cereals for _ _ _ _ _ _ _ _ _ _. **BREAKFAST**

SET OF QUESTIONS 7

FESTIVALS, NUMBERS (30-100) & RELATIVE'S AGE:

1. Follow the sequence: 100, 90, 80… **70, 60, 50…**
2. What do we celebrate on December 25th? **A) CHRISTMAS DAY**; B) FAMILY DAY; C) HALLOWEEN
3. How old is your grandfather? **HE IS (STUDENTS' OWN ANSWERS)**
4. What do you do at Easter? A) SING CAROLS; **B) DECORATE EGGS**; C) PUT UP THE CHRISTMAS TREE
5. What do we celebrate on March 17th? **A) ST. PATRICK'S DAY**; B) FRIENDSHIP DAY; C) INTERNATIONAL WOMEN'S DAY
6. Add 30 to 40, what number have you got? **70**
7. What word can you make using the first letter of each of the following words? **C**anada, **A**rgentina, **R**ed, **N**ine, **I**s, **V**acation, **A**nt, **L**ibrary. **CARNIVAL**
8. Subtract 10 from 50, what number have you got? **40**
9. Which is not a Halloween custome? A) GHOST; B) SKELETON; **C) PRINCESS**
10. How old is your mother/father? **SHE/HE IS (STUDENTS' OWN ANSWERS)**
11. How many hours are there in a day? **24**

SET OF QUESTIONS 8

SPORTS/ENTERTAINERS, CAN/CAN'T & POSSESSIVE PRONOUNS (HIS/HER):

1. What sport can you make out of these letters? G-S-M-M-I-W-N-I. **SWIMMING**
2. When do you usually go skiing? A) IN SUMMER; **B) IN WINTER**; C) IN AUTUMN; D) IN SPRING
3. Can your best friend do a cartwheel? **A) YES, SHE/HE CAN; B) NO, SHE/HE CAN'T (STUDENTS' OWN ANSWERS)**
4. What sport can you play with a small ball and a small racquet on a table? A) TENNIS; **B)TABLE TENNIS**; C) ROLLERBLADING
5. Do you…? **A) GO CLIMBING**; B) DO CLIMBING; C) PLAY CLIMBING
6. Unscramble the words in order to build a sentence: RIDING/HER/HORSE/SPORT/IS/FAVOURITE. **HORSE RIDING IS HER FAVOURITE SPORT**
7. What's your best friend's favourite sport? SAMPLE ANSWER: **HER/HIS FAVOURITE SPORT IS (STUDENTS' OWN ANSWERS)**
8. Complete the sentence: I _____ karate 3 days a week. **DO**
9. Can you juggle? A) YES, I CAN; B) NO, I CAN'T. **STUDENTS' OWN ANSWERS**
10. What word can you make out of these letters? B-D-S-A-K-T-E-A-R-O. **SKATEBOARD**
11. Can you do a handstand? A) YES, I CAN; B) NO, I CAN'T. **STUDENTS' OWN ANSWERS**

SET OF QUESTIONS 9

CLOTHES, SEASONS & PRESENT CONTINUOUS/ POSSESSIVE (saxon genitive):

1. What type of coat can I wear when it rains? **A RAINCOAT**
2. What is the person on your right wearing? **SHE'S/HE'S WEARING… (STUDENTS' OWN ANSWERS)**
3. What's the opposite of baggy? A) SHORT; **B) TIGHT**; C) SOFT
4. What type of print do flamenco dresses have on them? **A) SPOTTY**; B) STRIPY; C) SHORT
5. Can you name the 4 seasons? **SPRING, SUMMER, AUTUMN AND WINTER**
6. What do you wear in winter to protect your hands from cold weather? **GLOVES**
7. What do you wear in winter to protect your feet from cold weather? **SOCKS**
8. Rearrange the letters in order to make a word: P-A-C. **CAP**
9. What types of clothes do you wear over your legs? **JEANS / TROUSERS / SKIRT**
10. What colour are/is your teacher's trousers/skirt? **MY TEACHER'S TROUSERS/SKIRT ARE/IS… (STUDENTS' OWN ANSWERS)**
11. What clothes do you usually wear in summer? **STUDENTS' OWN ANSWERS**

SET OF QUESTIONS 10

FOOD & DRINKS, SEQUENCING (first, then, finally) & LIKE/HATE/LOVE:

1. Spot the odd one out: ORANGE-LEMON-**GREEN BEANS**
2. What do sweets contain? **SUGAR**
3. Name one ingredient to make a Spanish Omelette. **SAMPLE ANSWERS: POTATOES, EGGS, SALT, OLIVE OIL…**
4. What is the main ingredient of Paella? **RICE**
5. What type of foods are cheese, yoghurt or cream? A) CEREALS; **B) DAIRY PRODUCTS**; C) FRUIT
6. How often should we eat fat (fatty food such as hamburgers)? A) ALWAYS; **B) SOMETIMES**; C) OFTEN
7. Correct the sequence: (FOR LUNCH) FIRST I EAT FRUIT, THEN I EAT MEAT AND FINALLY I EAT VEGETABLES. **STUDENTS' OWN ANSWERS**
8. Which of the following do you like the most? Fish, meat or pasta. **STUDENTS' OWN ANSWERS**
9. What do I need to make a sandwich? A) SUGAR; **B) BREAD**; C) POTATOES
10. Correct the sequence: to cook chips… FIRST, I CUT THE POTATOES; THEN, I FRY THE POTATOES; FINALLY, I WASH THE POTATOES. **1ST WASH, 2ND CUT, 3RD FRY**
11. What type of food do you hate? **I HATE…(STUDENTS' OWN ANSWERS)**

SET OF QUESTIONS 11

CITY & COUNTRY PLACES, PREPOSITIONS & VERB TO BE (interrogative):

1. Where in the city shall I go if I want to watch a film? **TO THE CINEMA**
2. Spot the odd one out: A) AIRPORT; B) HOTEL; **C) MOUNTAIN**
3. Unscramble the letters in order to find a place in the city: M-M-U-E-S-U. **MUSEUM**
4. Where in the city shall I go if I want to do sports? **SPORTS CENTRE**
5. What's next to the sports centre in your town? **STUDENTS' OWN ANSWERS**
6. What's opposite the hospital in your town? **STUDENTS' OWN ANSWERS**
7. Say if the following sentence can be true or false: 'The Lake is in the theatre'. **FALSE**
8. What do we call a mountain with a circular hole at the top through which lava comes out? **VOLCANO**
9. What do we call a large body of ice moving slowly down a valley on a land surface? **GLACIER**
10. What are 'Júcar' and 'Huécar'? A) LAKES; **B) RIVERS**; C) THEATRES
11. Where in the city shall I go if I want to see the 'Lion King Musical'? **TO THE THEATRE**

SET OF QUESTIONS 12

CAMPING ITEMS, VERB TO HAVE GOT & PREPOSITIONS:

1. When going camping, where do we usually sleep? **IN A TENT**
2. What do I need to use to know where North is? **A COMPASS**
3. Have you got a first aid kit? **A) YES, I HAVE; B) NO I HAVEN'T. STUDENTS' OWN ANSWERS**
4. Rearrange the letters so as to find an instrument to cook in the countryside: CAMPING E-S-O-T-V. **STOVE**
5. Spot the odd one out: A) PICNIC SET; **B) INSECT REPELLENT**; C) PICNIC TABLE
6. What should we use so we don't get sunburnt? **SUNSCREEN**
7. What have you got in your backpack? **I'VE GOT…(STUDENTS' OWN ANSWERS)**
8. Do you sleep…? **A) IN THE TENT**; B) BEHIND THE TENT; C) UNDER THE TENT
9. What do you use to cover yourself while sleeping in the tent? **SLEEPING BAG**
10. What do you need to see at night? **A LANTERN**
11. What can you use a rope for? **STUDENTS' OWN ANSWERS**

Sobre la autora

Carolina Cubells García es Maestra de Educación Especial y Técnico Superior en Prevención de Riesgos Laborales en las especialidades de Ergonomía, Psicosociología y Seguridad en el Trabajo. Su trayectoria ha sido de lo más diversa, habiendo obtenido certificaciones tan dispares como la de Tripulante de Cabina de Pasajeros o el CPE_Cambridge (Certificate of Proficiency in English), nivel C2 según el MCER (Marco Común Europeo de Referencia para las lenguas) en 2019. La mayor parte de su trayectoria laboral ha estado ligada a la enseñanza de la lengua inglesa, así como a la del español como lengua extranjera. Accedió al cuerpo de maestros en Castilla la Mancha por la especialidad de inglés en el año 2022, ejerciendo su puesto en escuelas públicas de índole principalmente rural en dicha Comunidad Autónoma. Actualmente, Carolina compagina su actividad docente con una activa formación continua tanto en el área de la enseñanza como en el de la psicología transpersonal, campo que intenta integrar en sus propuestas didácticas.

Agradecimientos

A toda mi familia, y en particular a mis padres, por su apoyo incondicional.
A mi amante y amigo David, por ser una bonita luz y acompañarme en todas las pequeñas aventuras que van surgiendo en el camino.
A mis queridas amistades, por enseñarme a ser una mejor versión de mí misma.
Agradezco de manera muy especial a Victoria Arendasova, por haberme ayudado a crecer y a salir adelante cuando más lo he necesitado.
A Miriam Cotillas, por su dedicación, sus sugerencias y sabios consejos, que siempre me han impulsado a activar cambios y florecer.
A todos los estudiantes que van pasado por mi vida, por las enseñanzas genuinas que me van dejando.
A Andrea Rubio, paisana y antigua alumna, por sus bonitas ilustraciones.
A Sara Gómez, cuya maquetación inicial ha servido de gran ayuda para la elaboración de la actual.
A Julie-Anne Farman, por ayudarme a desoxidar mi inglés de vez en cuando, así como por su revisión del cuento.
A la editorial, por su paciente orientación y guía.
A ti, por haber adquirido este pequeño cuento. Espero que te sea útil.

¡Tu perspectiva es invaluable! A pesar de las múltiples revisiones, el ojo humano puede pasar por alto algunos detalles. Te agradecería enormemente que enviaras un e-mail a cubelinka@gmail.com si detectaras cualquier posible error o incluso si tuvieras alguna propuesta de mejora. ¡Gracias por tu colaboración!